THE TUI

We wish to express our appreciation for the many years of voluntary work done by the members of Native Bird Recovery Richmond. Everybody enjoys the improvement in native bird numbers, especially the Tuis, in Richmond.

Thanks go to Ewing Poultry for donating eggs for the stoat traps.
We've also appreciated support from Fresh Choice Richmond, Tasman District Council, BNZ and The Copy Press.

Cover design by Suzanne North

BOOKS
Published 2013
by Anne Webb and Neil Page with CP Books, Nelson, New Zealand

A4 version ISBN 978-0-473-25295-3

A5 version ISBN 978-0-473-27161-9

 Printed by The Copy Press, Nelson, New Zealand. www.copypress.co.nz

A Pictorial Study of New Zealand's colourful endemic bird
Produced by Anne Webb and Neil Page
as a fundraiser for Native Bird Recovery Richmond

Most New Zealanders think that their iconic native bird
the NZ Tui [*Prosthemadera novaeseelandiae*]
is just a black bird with a white tuft.

However, nothing could be further from the truth.
In fact it does not have a black feather on its body.
We would therefore like to introduce you to the very colourful and
multi-hued bird that the Tui really is.

The Tui can appear black to the observer because the feathers seem to have some form of iridescent coating that is able to defeat the optics of both the eye and the camera.

A particularly unique feature of the Tui is the white tuft under its chin. It has the appearance of a priestly dog collar and gives the Tui the common name of 'Parson Bird'.

Contrary to common perception, the tuft is not a single tuft,
but is instead two separate tufts that can move independently,
especially when vocalising.

Despite it being a unique and stand out feature the white collar
around the Tui's neck is not seen by most people.
That collar is made up of intricate white feathers, which give the
appearance of a delicate Victorian lace collar or shawl.

Another particular feature of the Tui is its articulated tongue, which gives it a very long reach for extracting nectar from deep throated flowers.

A further feature of the tongue is that the tip is fibrous like an artist's brush, which allows the Tui to use it like a sponge for drinking and soaking up nectar.

The Tui's diet consists of nectar, insects, fruits, and berries.
The bird's head is often brightly coloured by pollen.

The Tui has a very strong and sharp set of talons that it uses for clinging to things in difficult positions, even hanging upside down, to gather nectar from awkward places. While not normally used as offensive weapons those talons have been known to be employed very effectively in defense.

As both males and females have identical colouring, markings, and plumage, it is almost impossible to casually identify gender. The birds can only be positively identified by head size, measured from the back of the head to the tip of the beak. Males are larger than 59mm and females smaller.

Despite the Tui appearing to be a handsome, good mannered, well presented, sedate, and lady-like bird, it is in fact a solitary, rude, aggressive, dominating bully, that is particularly possessive of its immediate territory and food sources, chasing off all other comers.

When warning off or challenging any interlopers the Tui dramatically increases its size by puffing up its feathers to give the impression of being a far larger and more aggressive bird.

This behaviour is not just for show, as these challenges can, and do, often end up in very loud and physical pecking fights, with the loser being chased off, at high speeds, for a considerable distance.

The only exception to this aggressive behaviour is during the
spring mating season when the Tuis pair off.
They produce two to four eggs which incubate in fourteen days.

After hatching, the chicks take a further fourteen days to fledge and have a distinct juvenile plumage. They only start to develop the characteristic colouring, tufts, and collars as adolescents.

Tuis like to bathe and are frequently seen in suburban bird baths. They also 'shower' in the foliage of certain trees after rain.
They flap their wings and tumble in the water soaked leaves, using them as a natural spa.

When wet, the Tui can be seen imitating a wet dog,
to spin dry itself.

Tuis, like all birds, spend a great deal of time grooming,
in order to maintain a clean aerodynamic profile.
Oil is also distributed from a small gland on their back near the
tail in order to retain water resistance.

While the Tui is close to the top of the bird pecking order, it still
has its own predators, such as possums, stoats, ferrets, weasels,
rats, cats, and dogs, which either attack the birds directly
or eat their young and eggs.

This one legged poor fellow we called Hoppy.

As the light of day fades so does the Tui's rich technicolor display
and once again it becomes the commonly perceived
black bird with a white tuft.

The End

Native Bird Recovery Richmond [NBRR] is a small group of dedicated volunteers who trap predators in four bush gullies behind Richmond. Since 2005 they have trapped more than 6,300 pests. As a result the bird life has increased substantially. The volunteers also undertake noxious weed control and a native planting programme.

In 2010 NBRR constructed a hide beside the Jimmy Lee track above Hill St. This hide is for the public to view our native bird life up close because most people have never seen our iconic native birds from close quarters.

The Ornithological Society in conjunction with NBRR is also conducting a DOC approved study of the Tui's territorial habits. Almost 100 Tuis have been individually identified with bands and many of them are frequently seen throughout Richmond.

This pictorial study of the Tui was produced by Anne Webb and Neil Page to show off the Tui, our colourful endemic bird, in all its true glory, and as a fundraiser for NBRR.

The following people kindly allowed access to their properties for photography:

Tony and Shirley Jackson of Richmond
Maureen Schmidt of Richmond
Anne Webb of Ruby Bay
Neil Page of Richmond

NBRR thanks you for your support